PALM BEACH

FACES AND PLACES

CENTENNIAL 1911-2011

PALM BEACH

FACES AND PLACES

CENTENNIAL 1911-2011

STAR GROUP
INTERNATIONAL INC

StarGroup International, Inc.
West Palm Beach, Florida

Coordinated by Brenda Star

Designed & Photographed by Mel Abfier

Edited by Gwen Carden, Jane Evers and Jef Lawlor

Produced by StarGroup International, Inc.
www.stargroupinternational.com
561.547.0667

Library of Congress Card Number: Pending

PALM BEACH - FACES AND PLACES
Centennial 1911-2011
ISBN 978-1-884886-95-9

SPONSORS

The Breakers Palm Beach
Grand Sponsor

The Fanjul Family

Lawrence A. Moens Associates, Inc.

William Pitt Foundation

The Honorable Lesly S. Smith

Palm Beach Daily News

FOREWORD

Having lived and worked in Palm Beach for more than 25 years, it gives me great pleasure to share some of its rich history and gracious charm, with residents and visitors alike, as we celebrate the Palm Beach Centennial in 2011!

Palm Beach – Faces and Places is a collection of candid memories and photographs that embody the essence of this enchanting, storied island community. At the center of everything Palm Beach is the iconic Breakers Hotel, created in 1896 by our visionary founder, Henry Flagler. Thanks to members of the Kenan family, descendants of Flagler's wife, Mary Lily Kenan, The Breakers continues to represent so many fine qualities for which this special town is known.

As the Town of Palm Beach enters into its next 100 years, we look forward to carrying on the tradition of gracious hospitality with our neighbors and guests alike.

Paul N. Leone

President
The Breakers Palm Beach

PREFACE

Fascinating how an opportune planting of washed-ashore coconuts from a ship wreck attracted a visionary and dreamer and a golden resort sprang to life. This vision would be the beginning of an international resort that became an icon of Patrician style. A town whose history and heritage of fame that would attract many visionaries and dreamers.

My earliest memory of Palm Beach is its beauty, neatness and color. I feel tenderness and appreciation of my good fortune to live here, completely surrounded by water that continually reflects the facets of its beauty, bright sky, pleasure and privilege.

I thank all the contributors who brought the past to the present by helping make this Centennial book memorable and valuable by sharing their memories, events, and thoughts. This is a commerative book with the patina of what we have become.

While Palm Beach stands alone in its uniqueness, it is important to remember that its existence is fragile. A quote from Giuseppe Tomasi di Lampedusa's novel *The Leopard* says, "If we want things to stay as they are, things will have to change." That change is our challenge for the next 100 years. As we celebrate now, let us hope that the past is prologue.

Jack McDonald
Mayor of Palm Beach

CENTENNIAL CELEBRATION

Palm Beach got its name from the coconut palms that blanketed the shores of Lake Worth after the Spanish ship Providencia wrecked here in 1893. The beauty of sky and sea, the perfect winter climate, the eclectic architecture and lush gardens, both public and private, combine to make Palm Beach a place of unique beauty. However, it is the people who make Palm Beach like no other place in all the world.

Henry Flagler, co-founder with John D. Rockefeller of the Standard Oil Company, was the first man of vision and resources to bring the world's most wealthy and beautiful people to Palm Beach. Since his time, this town has received kings and presidents, titans of industry, stars of stage and screen, billionaires and scoundrels; yet even more interesting than the famous and infamous are the elegant people and friendly faces seen here every day.

This year marks the 100th anniversary of the founding of the Town of Palm Beach. Who are the people of Palm Beach and what makes where they live so special? Flip the pages of this book and experience paradise through the camera lens of noted photographer Mel Abfier and the creative energy of Brenda Star.

Bill Bone

Chairman
Palm Beach Centennial Commission

INTRODUCTION

This book was one of those "last minute ideas" that was just too good to pass up. What could be more fitting for the Palm Beach Centennial than to create a book which would be a snapshot of today's Palm Beach with a few thoughts from today's Palm Beachers? Could we really pull everything together in less than two months….for a project that could easily take a year? After the idea was ignited, Paul Leone, President of The Breakers Palm Beach, encouraged us to make it happen and took a leadership role as The Grand Sponsor of the project. We quickly extended an open invitation to the community requesting their thoughts and memories. The Chamber of Commerce, The Civic Association, the Palm Beach Daily News and many other business associations helped get the word out. The grapevine of phone calls and e-mails grew throughout the town. Mayor Jack McDonald even escorted us up and down Worth Avenue for our first photo shoot! So many wonderful people helped pave our way to move quickly. The good news is that we did it! The not-so-good news is that everybody didn't get the message in time to be included. We wish we had had more time to gather even more fun memories and images. I think we captured the essence of what it is like to live in Palm Beach, one of the most incredible, beautiful and unique towns in the world. Enjoy!

Brenda Star

President
StarGroup International, Inc.

SPECIAL THANKS

We thank the many people who helped make this book a reality… the cheerleaders, the messengers, the authors, and the models who helped showcase a "day in the life of Palm Beach" and who helped pay tribute to the Palm Beach Centennial. Those who did not appear should not be considered any less important than those that did. Omissions may have been due to tight schedule conflicts and/or time constraints. Special thanks to the sponsors… The Breakers Palm Beach, The Fanjul Family, Lawrence A. Moens Associates, Inc., William Pitt Foundation, The Honorable Lesly S. Smith and Palm Beach Daily News who helped make the book available to the community for the 2011 Centennial celebrations. For the wonderful photography, creative design, support and patience (!)… an "extra" special thanks goes to Mel Abfier, Creative director of StarGroup International.

Brenda Star

I've traveled widely, but I am not aware of another city in the world, or even a small district in a city, that so beautifully and economically compresses so much timeless architecture, landscape artistry and ocean view, culinary delights, history, art, interesting and mostly quite wonderful people into such an unforgettable creation and fantasy, painstakingly preserved.

This is our Palm Beach, our shining gem by the sea.

James Patterson
Resident Novelist

On the centennial of The Breakers in 1996, our Chairman, James G. Kenan, III wrote, "we hope that The Breakers will continue to be as special for our guests today and tomorrow as it has been in years past. The Breakers centennial book tells a great history, but perhaps the best is yet to come". I share James Kenan's sentiments and feel the best is yet to come for the town of Palm Beach.

For all of its history and grandeur, one of the best things about Palm Beach is the small town feel, where you can walk the streets, know all your neighbors, and raise a family. Thanks to our affiliation with The Breakers and the Kenan family, Kathy and I feel blessed to have been able to raise our four sons, Ben, Griffin, Jake and Nicky, in the comfort of this gracious, generous, beautiful seaside town.

Paul N. Leone
Resident

I've been associated with Palm Beach for over 50 years. My husband Bob Davidoff started his photography business here in 1959. Our first studio was on Bradley Place where Publix now stands.

In the summertime the traffic lights on Sunrise and Bradley were taken down. The Paramount building hosted charity events attended by many stars.

Our first winter we rented a cottage behind a home rented by Cloris Leachman. My boys and hers played together. One day my son Ken came home and said she had company, a man who liked to play bongos. Turned out to be Marlon Brando!

Babe Davidoff
Davidoff Studios

W hen I came to Palm Beach to work on the Kravis Center project 21 years ago, I was struck by the physical beauty of Palm Beach and the friendliness of everyone I met. The memory of that first early gala at The Breakers where the model was unveiled for what would become The Raymond F. Kravis Center for the Performing Arts is still a fond and thrilling one. More than 800 people attended. Twenty one years later, Palm Beachers are still among our best ambassadors for arts and culture throughout the county.

Judith A. Mitchell

*Raymond F. Kravis Center for the
Performing Arts*

Visiting the Four Arts Garden gives us a sense of continuity and connection to the early days of our town. The garden was planted in 1938 as seven small demonstration gardens created by members of The Garden Club of Palm Beach to show what could be grown here. Ever since, our club members have maintained this beautiful, peaceful place mindful of those who came before us as well as of those yet to come.

Betsy Matthews, Cindy Hoyt, Jean Matthews, Heather Henry

The Garden Club of Palm Beach

My favorite thing to do in Palm Beach is walk east down Worth Avenue on a cool, sunny winter day when the sky is an amazing color of blue, only topped by the deep blue of the ocean. The shop windows create a fairyland of worldly goods, and smiles and greetings fill everyone with good cheer. A parade of beautiful cars and beautiful people cruises down the avenue. It's the "season" in Palm Beach, and I can't think of anywhere quite like it.

Judi Miracle Richards

Resident

Cindy Hoyt, Jean Matthews, Heather Henry and Betsy Matthews

I love the rich cultural life offered in Palm Beach through the Society of the Four Arts, the Palm Beach Symphony, the Kravis Center, the Norton Museum, Ann Norton Museum, Florida Stage, Dramaworks, the Armory, galleries and more.

In the many years the Liman Gallery has been in the historic Paramount Building, which has a wonderful "museum" of movie memorabilia, I have seen not only this growth but have been lucky enough to collaborate with many talented artists. Palm Beach is a stimulating cultural environment for artists and audiences alike.

Ellen Liman
Liman Gallery

I have been fortunate to be a part of Palm Beach since 2003 and love everything about it - the charm, the beach, the lifestyle, the hedges, all of it! It is exciting to know that through 100 years of history this beautiful island and oasis has evolved.

Deborah Carr
Omphoy Ocean Resort

My favorite memory is returning to Palm Beach and driving over the bridge feeling so proud to be part of this unique oasis. My favorite people are all those who truly appreciate what we were and what we are and want to preserve it. My favorite thing to do is anything in our special relaxed and charming atmosphere. What I love most about Palm Beach is that it has remained true to its identity, developed and nurtured by devoted residents who appreciated our incredible legacy. I hope Palm Beach remains true to itself for the next 100 years.

The Honorable Yvelyne deMarcellus "Deedy" Marix
Former Mayor

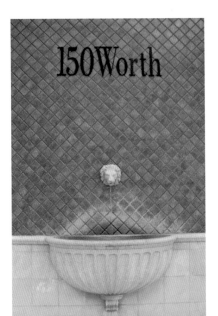

Franklyn DeMarco

Acquiring a lot at 221 Worth Avenue, Palm Beacher Ted Stone developed the building which would become Ta-boó. In the fall of 1941 as the restaurant neared completion friends began discussing names.

You should call it___, offered one fellow. That's obscene, you can't call it that, replied a pal.

You should call it ____, suggested another. That's too bawdy, it will offend people, another critic retorted.

You should call it _____, offered one wild rascal. Oh no, that's Ta-boó, was the unanimous reply. Well, said Stone, we'll name it Ta-boó.

The name has stuck ever since.

Franklyn DeMarco
Ta-boó

Some of my favorite times was being involved with sports activities and coaching little league baseball with the youngsters from the Day School, the public school and the Recreation Center.

And, what could have been more fun than the Sunday Rolls Royce Parade down Worth Avenue in my '39 Silver Wraith with the Palm Beach Rolls Royce gang!?!

Murray Goodman

Resident

I vividly recall traveling from Virginia to vacation with my parents as a young boy in a magical place known as Palm Beach. Later, as a student, I was introduced to Bloody Marys at the Loggia Lounge and absolutely loved having vichyssoise and a Caesar salad for lunch at Petite Marmite. And, to even things out, I also spent thoughtful, spiritual moments at Bethesda-by-the-Sea Episcopal Church. It was, and still is, a memorable, life-altering experience.

Charles James Frankel III

Retired, Cypress Trust Company

Murray and Joanie Goodman

Bill Koch
America's Cup winner, 1992

My family and I left Cuba in 1959 and arrived in Palm Beach to wait for Castro to fall. We thought that communism and the dictatorship never would survive just 90 miles from the greatest country in the world - we were wrong!

We were right, however, to make Palm Beach our home. How lucky can we be to have our whole family living in a place like this! We are eternally grateful to this country and everyone here who received us with open arms and gave us the support we needed. It's been a wonderful 50 years.

Alfonso "Alfy" Fanjul

Florida Crystals

Living in Palm Beach creates an intimate feeling. No matter where you go, you run into someone you know.

My wife and I love to sit and read by the pool, overlooking the ocean. Most activities are within minutes of our home including the chapel, shopping on Worth Avenue and restaurants. The security and privacy supplied by our police department and fire rescue is outstanding.

Llwyd Ecclestone

Resident

I moved Photo Electronics Corporation from the Northeast to the Palm Beaches 42 years ago. Seeing a need for a stronger cultural community, a group of us founded the Arts Council (now the Cultural Council). As Founding Chairman, I helped raise $63 million to build the Raymond F. Kravis Center for the Performing Arts. Today the community's cultural institutions make it attractive to highly educated people, such as those doing research at Scripps and Max Planck.

Alex Dreyfoos

Founding Chairman (Retired)
Raymond F. Kravis Center for the Performing Arts

Alfonso " Alfy" Fanjul, Llwyd Ecclestone and Alex Dreyfoos

I moved to Palm Beach in 1982 with three children under age four, not knowing a soul. The Seaview Park Recreation Center was my refuge for finding playmates for my children and an opportunity to meet other moms. Back then the playground was just a sandbox and old swing set and slide. Over the last 29 years, the Recreation Center has transformed with the addition of a multi-purpose building, eight lighted tennis courts and a deluxe playground that accommodates both adults and children. Its spell has enchanted a new generation. I proudly call it one of my favorite places.

Gail Coniglio
Resident and Town Council Member

After a 25-day sail from Gibraltar, I was greeted by my wife Etonella at the seawall of The Breakers Hotel at 8:15 a.m. Etonella was attending a Chamber breakfast in the Venetian Room. Using my loud hailer, I requested she get home quickly, since I hadn't seen her for two months. When she entered the Venetian Room, everyone clapped and laughed, as my voice had carried through the windows. Chairman Jesse Newman announced that Etonella could speak first, considering that she had a pressing engagement at home.

John C. Christlieb
Resident

Gail Coniglio
with grandchildren, Topher, Piper and Nicholas

I love the island's physical beauty. From the striking vistas of the Atlantic Ocean and the Intracoastal to the fabulous gardens of the Four Arts Sculpture Garden, Pan's Garden and the Earl T. Smith Garden, each offers a wondrous gift of beauty, both man-made and natural.

I love the sense of historical perspective in our architecture as evidenced in the wonderful old mansions, the charm of our "Sea" Street neighborhoods, and landmarked buildings such as Town Hall, Mar-a-Lago, St. Edwards Catholic Church, and The Breakers. Worth Avenue's recent renovation shows respect for the past while building for the future.

Richard M. Kleid

Palm Beach Town Councilman

My best memories of Palm Beach were the times I took my young twin sons Chad and Christian to the Clarke Avenue beach and we surfed together on our long boards. The spring evening surf was always perfect, and the water was crystal clear and turquoise.

We also enjoyed fishing on the lake and investigating the Palm Beach shoreline and mangrove islands in our small boat. We were alone together under God's creation.

Chauncey Crandall, M.D.

Resident

Bruce Strickland and Norbert Goldner

P alm Beach is no longer just a terminal on the Flagler Railroad, it's a place in our hearts...a true paradise.

The Honorable Lesly S. Smith

Former Mayor

I never miss the tree lighting on Worth Avenue. My first year in Florida, a friend invited me to attend the tree lighting. Coming from big city Philadelphia, it was really wonderful to see so many town residents coming out to share in the celebration. It is always a fantastic way to kick off the holiday season with friends and family.

Michael J. Dixon
Carl Domino, Inc.

I'm proud of my family's long association with the Town of Palm Beach. My 98-year-old mother's uncle, Leo Gerstenzang, who invented the Q-Tip, first came to winter in Palm Beach in the early 1940s. Later, his widow Zuita Akston built a magnificent home on the lake known as "La Ronda," where I stayed for many a season. Unfortunately "La Ronda" was demolished a few years ago, but Aunt Zuita's gift to Palm Beach, known as the Noguchi sculpture "Tetra," still stands on Four Arts Plaza where it can be seen by everyone coming across the middle bridge into the town.

Bill Diamond
Resident & Palm Beach Town Councilman

Palm Beach is a magical place. The sun shines every day, even when it rains. The real Islanders have known each other for generations. It is the beach, the palm trees, the fountains and three-toed cats, Lilly Pulitzer, and knowing tomorrow will be just as wonderful as today!

Colleen Orrico
C. Orrico

The best thing about Palm Beach is its wonderful small town feeling. Even though not all of the residents live here year-round, you soon recognize and get to know everyone. Having only one grocery store and one drugstore helps make that happen!

Barbara and Irvin Saltzman

Residents

Michael J. Dixon, Barbara and Irvin Saltzman

Bill and Kit Pannill with Talbott Maxey

P alm Beach is a warm and welcoming place. We have lived in our house on Lake Worth for 24 years. We love walking or biking on the bike path. My favorite place is the Society of the Four Arts. The Four Arts Garden maintained by the Garden Club of Palm Beach is the most beautiful garden in Palm Beach.

Kit and Bill Pannill

Residents

Bob and Ed Kassatly

When we were kids our dad would take us to ride the Afromobiles... what fun!

Bob and Ed Kassatly

Kassatly's

I love how much Palm Beach is about family. I have raised my two boys here... started a store with my sisters... had my parents on the sales floor... and people here don't just understand, they embrace that. That kind of love and bond is what makes the island such a welcoming place to be, and the style so easy.

Casey Orrico

C. Orrico

Riding my bike on the Lake Trail is the best thing to do in Palm Beach. Known as the "earliest street" because it was created by Henry Flagler in 1894 as a strolling path for guests of the Royal Poinciana Hotel, it now stretches nine miles alongside the Intracoastal Waterway on the west and has some of the world's most beautiful private residences on the east. I jokingly call it the Trail of Conspicuous Consumption for the magnificent mansions, artwork and gardens occasionally glimpsed through or above the perfectly manicured hedges. The Lake Trail is a joy day or night.

Bill Bone
Resident

In 1947 my family was living on Oleander Avenue, and I was a student at Palm Beach High School. During that summer I worked at the Sun and Surf Club, now the site of the Sun and Surf Condominiums. My job was taking care of the tennis courts. The club was part of the Whitehall Hotel.

There were five movie theaters in West Palm Beach, all downtown. I would walk to the Biltmore which was then a hotel and pay five cents to take a small passenger ferry to the foot of First Street to go to the movies.

Elliot H. Klorfein, M.D.
Resident

Bill Bone with Carlton and Rex

As a young child my mother, twin brother and I often visited Worth Avenue. We'd go into Gallery Juarez and get to walk the owner's two standard poodles, which were as big as we were. We were quite a sight barreling down Worth Avenue with those dogs.

We also shopped at the Lullaby Shop and Prep Shop, where our store is located today. When we renovated that space we discovered that the famous Lullaby murals were still there. We left them untouched within our new walls. Someday someone will get a marvelous surprise when they renovate.

Stefan Richter
Richters of Palm Beach

I love the mornings in Palm Beach, a time when the sun comes up on the Atlantic, the streets are empty, and I feel like I have Palm Beach all to myself.

John Maus

Maus and Hoffman

John Maus

When we left Cuba in 1959, our family was warmly welcomed into this great country. Our close-knit happy family was privileged to make Palm Beach our home. Our business was re-established here providing us with a platform for growth. Palm Beach is a paradise and a total contrast from life in communist Cuba. Some of my happiest memories are in this special place we have called home for over fifty years. Thank you, Palm Beach!

Emilia and Pepe Fanjul, Sr.

Residents

We are thankful everyday to live in such a special place, where we are surrounded by our family and close friends. We are blessed to be able to call Palm Beach our home.

Lourdes and Pepe Fanjul, Jr.

Residents

Lourdes and Pepe Fanjul, Jr. with LuLu and Peps

Emilia and Pepe Fanjul, Sr.

It was a Sunday afternoon in 1973 right after the movie "Jaws" was released. I was on Clarke Avenue Beach when a big shark fin was spotted. Everyone ran out of the water screaming and lined up along the shore. Police sharpshooters came to the scene. It turned out to be a hoax when the fin washed up on shore. It was quite the story and appeared on the front page of the newspaper.

Dale R. Hedrick

Hedrick Brothers Construction

Dale Hedrick & Gene Parker

There is much to love about the paradise that is Palm Beach. Both style and substance complete the rich landscape. The style reminds me of the Great Gatsby replete with dapper men and elegantly jeweled women set against a backdrop of ornate Mizner architecture on piercing turquoise waters with mystical banyans and lush foliage adding to the island's allure. This and the substantial philanthropic endeavors of the people of Palm Beach is inspiring. For these myriad reasons, I am proud and honored to call Palm Beach "Home".

Harold F. Corrigan

Candlewood Consultants

Sherry Frankel and Marley Herring

As a resident of Palm Beach for 15 years I still consider the island a fantasy island, like no place on the planet. As this grande dame approaches her 100th birthday I remember a time when all the shops closed on Sunday – including Publix. But as more people discovered this gem, the business community responded to their needs and not only began opening on Sunday but stayed open throughout the summer season.

Sherry Frankel

Sherry Frankel's Melangerie

I have fond memories of surfing on Dunbar Road as a teenager. Now I can sit back and watch the new generation of Palm Beachers continue that legacy.

What I love about Palm Beach is the beautiful tropical laid-back atmosphere and transitional slow growth of the last 50 years that has enhanced the island and community.

Robert Horner

Boynton Landscape Company

P alm Beach is paradise with the most beautiful beaches, homes, shopping, weather and warm people. The town was so special I produced a documentary about it entitled, "Palm Beach People and Places."

Dame Celia Lipton Farris

Resident

Mark Hassell
Ocean Rescue Supervisor

When I first came to Palm Beach in the late 1940s, I found the most wonderful and unusual people, so different than I expected. They were absolutely delightful!

Having an active roll in politics and charitable organizations has been a most rewarding life for me and, I hope, useful for others.

Helen Cluett

Resident

About twenty years ago a group of us organized the Palm Beach Fellowship of Christians and Jews. At that time there were many people who felt unaccepted in Palm Beach. I think there has been great progress through the efforts of good people working in the houses of worship and in organizations like The Fellowship to gain understanding and tolerance. Palm Beach is a wonderful place to live and I love it here.

Herb Lee
Resident

Palm Beach is a little pocket of Europe within our shores boasting beautiful architecture and exquisite sub-tropical vegetation along stretches of endless beach leading out to diamonds on the ocean. Nowhere else can you find such an amazing harmony of culture, commerce, philanthropy, education, sports and nature, all blended to form a magnificent mosaic that dazzles the senses. I awake each morning and give thanks that I am able to live in a heavenly paradise while still on earth!

Lexye Aversa

Professional Touch International

What I love about living and working in Palm Beach is that it can be whatever you want it to be - social, charitable or simply enjoyable with offerings like the wonderful Lake Trail, the beaches and the architecture.

My favorite person was Jesse Newman, the best "ambassador" the Town will ever have. We are also very lucky to have Jim Ponce as our historian extraordinaire.

Layne D. Nisenbaum, D.O.

Island Dermatology Laser & Anti-Aging Institute

Our family visited Palm Beach for 30 years before becoming Palm Beach residents. Now, as our home, my wife Lydia and I enjoy ocean walks, swimming, golf, dance lessons, and poetry-inspiring days in this earthly paradise. To live in a town with such natural beauty, good neighbors and good works is a blessing.

Robert L. Forbes

Resident

Robert L. Forbes

My memories of Palm Beach go back to the early Fifties. I remember Lido Pools, Wert's and the restaurant at the Palm Beach Pier.

In the Seventies we purchased a lot on North Woods Road at Woods Landing to build our home. Several people told me that they remember fishing there when it was Merrill's Landing. We are still living in that house.

Fruema Nannis Klorfein

Resident

Cyclists pass and say hello; police officers drive past and wave, neighbors walk their dogs. Palm Beach is at its most beautiful. For years I was a city person. I lived in New York, London, Sydney and Yerevan. But Palm Beach is where I look at trees, admire the water and hear the birds. There's no panacea for hustle like this island. In the evenings strangers sometime approach. "You're the lady I see walking every morning." And I imagine them standing at their windows, sipping coffee, and thinking: "There she goes again!"

Julia Harley-Green

Resident

Living on Seaspray Avenue in the center of town was wonderful. The Sea streets comprise a real neighborhood – with an energy and spirit of their own. The small-town charm was reflected in the architecture, the gardens and the people. This was a down-to-earth neighborhood where you really did know the folks on the street – and their children and their pets. The rhythm of the street was felt in the eclectic variety of architectural styles and roof lines. Children laughed, and long-time residents embraced the newcomers. It was a very good life filled with cherished memories.

Laurel Baker

Palm Beach Chamber of Commerce

Fun and fantastic Palm Beach memories continue to be in the making for me all the time. The most recent was getting to meet with so many of the wonderful people who generously shared their thoughts with us for this book. As the reminiscing began, inevitably, a big warm smile would follow!

Brenda Star

StarGroup International

Laurel Baker and Brenda Star

I remember when they were pumping mud off the bottom of Lake Worth and filled in Everglades Island. There were just boards where the bridge now stands. As a kid, I used to hunt with my 22 short along the mangroves. That area is now Flagler Drive. I also remember in the 60s when I attended my first town council meeting. It lasted one and a half minutes. Mayor Reese (wonderful man) took care of everything! I have seen lots and lots of changes over the years. What a place!

George Matthews
Resident

The most fascinating thing about Palm Beach's history is that it is so short. I've been able to talk to the children and grandchildren of some of the pioneers; people like Frank Hennessey, Flagler's last office boy, who told stories of life on the island when Flagler was still here. I even had a few words with Colonel Bradley, enabling me to get some idea of what it was really like during the heyday of its beginning.

I was surprised to hear it was also the 100th anniversary of the first airplane to fly over Palm Beach.

Jim Ponce

The Breakers Palm Beach Historian

My favorite Palm Beach event was the Festival of the Animals organized by the Hibel Museum to benefit children. I loved seeing the children and their parents enjoying the art, music, educational activities and animals. I especially enjoyed face painting the children, dressed as a clown.

My favorite people were Ginger Rogers and Julie Harris, who always visited me when in town.

I loved how the police watched over my mother Lena when she worked in my gallery. She enjoyed walking up and down Worth Avenue in the late evening, and a policeman would always ask how she was doing.

Edna Hibel

Internationally Reknowned Artist

Jim Ponce

Over 30 years ago I moved my family from New York City to this idyllic island. While outsiders viewed Palm Beach as a place of retirement and charitable parties we locals knew this was a place of opportunity.

We participated in transforming Palm Beach from a town that rolled up the sidewalks and implemented blinking traffic lights in summer to a vibrant full-time community. Palm Beach is a place where great leaders of culture, business and even countries mingle on a finite piece of real estate unlike anywhere else. There's simply no other place on earth like Palm Beach.

Garrison Lickle
Chilton Trust Management

To most non-residents Palm Beach is a glamorous oasis with innumerable galas and social climbers. That picture is not the reality. Palm Beach is a clean, safe, respectful and beautiful community, populated by accomplished, successful, non-publicity-seeking individuals who enjoy the island's many amenities ranging from the recreational facilities to the cultural opportunities. To prove my point just look at the board of the Civic Association composed almost exclusively of the more typical resident described above. I love not only the town but the residents.

Stanley M. Rumbough, Jr.
Resident

I have been associated with Palm Beach for 35 years, but my wife, Joanna, beats me by almost twofold. She remembers a town of subdued glitz, no multiple-story condominiums, a pier at the eastern end of Worth Avenue, and scrubland over the southern one-fifth of the town.

Palm Beach was unique then. Changes have occurred. However, thanks to judicious leaders, the town's development over time has been different from that of most other worldwide coastal resorts, because changes have been measured and thoughtful. It continues to be unique now and a joy to its residents.

Louis C. Pryor
Resident

Civic Association Directors
Brian McIver, Llwyd Ecclestone, Gary Lickle, Louis Pryor, Isabel Furlaud, Stan Rumbough

My favorite memory of Palm Beach is the beautiful night at Mar-a-Lago when Donald and I were married.

Melania Trump

Resident

My most vivid memory of Palm Beach was in 1985 when I first saw Mar-a-Lago. It was in disrepair, but I could see what a treasure it was.

Working on Mar-a-Lago was a labor of love for me. The amount of detail that went into its construction was an inspiration – both to match as well as to exceed.

The Department of the Interior designated the estate as the "Mar-a-Lago Historic Site" in 1969. It's the last remaining Palm Beach estate still containing its buildings and land in almost the identical form as its original conception. However, it's a work in progress and I've made many significant improvements in addition to the restoration. I remain loyal to the original vision and integrity of the estate, and I believe it's more beautiful than ever.

Donald J. Trump

Resident

Donald, Melania and Barron Trump

Now and then, when I find myself caught up in the daily grind, I drive down South Ocean Boulevard and look at the water. Sometimes there are kite-boarders out there, turning somersaults and flips in the wind or surfers balancing like tightrope walkers on the tips of waves. Sometimes the beach is empty and it's just miles and miles of ocean without a spec of a human being in sight. I'm never disappointed and I'm always grateful to be reminded of one of the many things that make living in Palm Beach so special.

Mary Simses
Resident

I'm mesmerized by Palm Beach's lush natural beauty and pristine beaches. The eclectic architectural styles that define the neighborhoods and the majesty of our landmarks never cease to awe me. I delight in the grandeur of strolling down "the Avenue" and the comfort of the folksiness of the mom & pop shops. I love Stubbs and Wootton accessorized tuxedos and fearless, Lilly colored everything, but I remain grateful to and inspired by this amazing community that celebrates the greatness of vision, the spirit of adventure and the importance of philanthropic commitment while remaining true to its small town feel.

Cynthia Rosa
Hamburger Heaven

M y favorite memory has to be the magical weekend of Donald and Melania Trump's wedding.

Bob Moore

Former Director of Planning, Zoning and Building Department

Bob Moore, Robert & Mary Simses with daughter, Morgan and Cindy Rosa

What I love about Palm Beach is its preservation of beauty and commitment to landmark architecture. I consider it to be one of the most beautiful urban locations in the world.

Palm Beach has a community memory that distinguishes it from other towns. It respects tradition and strives to conserve and appreciate its past.

Palm Beach satisfies our human need for stability and permanence while providing excitement and romance – and Palm Beach remains one of the few towns in America where you can wear a jacket and tie to dinner.

Jack McDonald

Mayor of Palm Beach

Palm Beach is more than architecture, landscaping, shopping, dining and the home of billionaires. It's a small town with residents whose spirit and generosity permeate the town. We extend our profound gratitude and admiration to the wonderful men and women who, in the past 100 years, with wisdom and integrity, provided a legacy for us to enjoy and pass on.

David A Rosow

President of the Town Council

Jack McDonald

We love Palm Beach because it is where our family is and has been since the late 1800s. We have a long history in Palm Beach and a love for the town. There is no other place we would want to call home. It's a great place to live and raise a family!

Richard and Pat Johnson

Resident

My fondest memory of Palm Beach will always be the Bethesda-by-the Sea Church. During the Christmas season, life-size figures of the Nativity scene are placed around the front and side of the church. Each night someone moves the camels, sheep, shepherds and The Three Wise Men closer to the manger. One day I said to my husband, "Steve, are those figures moving?" Then he noticed it, too. By the 25th of December the wise men and all the animals are around the manger. It's quite wonderful to watch.

Donna Dellaquila

Resident

Richard & Pat Johnson with Reverend Perry Fuller

Palm Beach has been my home for 24 years where I've met many fascinating people from all over the world. One early memory, when I learned to scuba dive, I discovered a Rolls Royce purposely dropped into the ocean to serve as a man-made reef and diver attraction right offshore. I was amazed that a diver could actually get behind the wheel of a car 60 feet below sea level. I knew from that moment that the magic and style of Palm Beach was to surprise and delight all those who stepped foot on her soil - including me.

Denise Bober

Palm Beach Chamber of Commerce

As a child I lived on the island with my grandparents during the winter months of 1960-1965 and attended services at the Royal Poinciana Chapel. Then, as now, I sensed an uncanny ease, affection and bond with Palm Beach, where I work and worship.

Adelene Keeler Smith

Interior Designer & Author

The Palm Beach memories I will always cherish are special times spent with my very special friends: Jesse Newman, Jack McDonald and Bob Moore. We shared an incredible weekly roundtable of friendship, laughter and stories, never discussing work or business. We enjoyed being together, having fun and bringing happiness to each other. We were like kids in a candy store. It makes me smile just thinking about it. We miss Jesse so much.

George Sharoubim

Giorgio's of Palm Beach

One can walk for miles and never see the same sight twice. The beach is a glorious vista in which I can meditate. The bike path, a beautiful place to exercise and view nature's wonders. The shops are filled with magnificent items. I enjoy reading at The Four Arts Library and love the beautiful Chinese gardens there. The Breakers Hotel never ceases to take my breath away.

Everywhere I go, whether it is in restaurants or shops, friendly people say hello. Palm Beach is a magical "small town" filled with tropical island delights!

Dr. Susan Lee

Florida Postgraduate Training Institute

George Sharoubim

I came to Palm Beach 45 years ago from Germany. Since the first day, I was fascinated by a house on the corner of Brazilian Avenue and South County Road. I was amused that you literally had to drive around the house to continue down South County Rd. In 1987 a dream came true when I purchased it. On closing day all I could think about was Kenny Rogers' song "The Gambler." "You never count your money when you're sittin' at the table. There'll be time enough for countin' when the dealin's done." And it was done with champagne.

Margrit Bessenroth
Resident

I remember when The Colony Hotel was only open during the Season. Each Season began the Monday before Thanksgiving with the Big Band Sounds of Marshall Grant or Alex Donner. All the ladies got a flower at the opening and a flower at the closing, which was the Monday after Mother's Day.

Bunnie Stevens
Resident

Captain Darrell Hayman
Dock Master, Sailfish Club of America

Ray Floyd
World Golf Hall of Fame Inductee

My favorite memory of Palm Beach was the re-opening of the Par 3 in December 2009 after two and a half years of planning, fundraising, and construction. This was a great example of the community pulling together for a very special Town facility.

My favorite person from Palm Beach is Henry Flagler, whose vision I admire.

My favorite thing to do here is enjoy our many great restaurants, and what I most love is being part of a small town community where everything is so convenient.

Raymond Floyd

World Golf Hall of Fame Inductee

Serving the town for the past five years as Director of Recreation (and now as the town's facilitator for the Centennial celebration) has provided me the privilege of working closely with numerous residents on a variety of projects.

Palm Beach's community spirit is obvious. I am most impressed with the high level of civic responsibility and citizen participation in town affairs. I believe this community to be truly special because of the excellent teamwork that exists among residents, businesses, community organizations and the town's employees.

Jay Boodheshwar

Recreation Director
Town of Palm Beach

I enjoy the relationship that we have with all of the churches and synagogues in town. The parishioners of St. Edward's Church are a source of happiness and inspiration to me.

Reverend Francis J. Lechiara

Resident

Palm Beach Kindergarten Soccer League

Dan Minic & Kevin Brandel, (tennis pros)
with the ladies from the Power Hour Clinic

I n 1978 we bought Gurnee Munn's home on North Lake Way. That year my mom stayed with us for the Season. One night she said that while biking she'd met "the vicar" and had tea with him. Had she biked all the way to Bethesda-by-the-Sea? "No," she said, "he lives right here on North Lake Way." She saw a sign outside a home saying "The Vicarage," rang the bell and was invited for afternoon tea with Douglas Fairbanks Jr. We all became friends and had many more teas with him and his wife Mary.

Etonella Christlieb
Resident

My favorite memories involve Easter in Palm Beach with my family - shopping on Worth Avenue, dinner at Chuck & Harold's, ice cream at Sprinkles, shopping at C. Orrico, hours of beach time at The Beach Club, Easter Mass at St. Edwards, and the Easter egg hunt at Seaview.

Kipper Lance
Resident

As a historian, I find it interesting that famed Palm Beach architect Addison Mizner built a connecting bridge between his home and office on Worth Avenue whose design was inspired by an infamous bridge in Europe called "The Bridge of Sighs". The Bridge of Sighs at one time in history took prisoners from the courts of Venice, Italy to dark holding cells.

Cynthia Morrison

British Auto

Palm Beach simply has everything… wonderful weather, world class shopping and restaurants and The Breakers, the best resort hotel in the world.

It doesn't get as hot here as many people think, because of the ocean and lake breezes. We are generally five degrees cooler than our neighboring communities, and we have very few mosquitoes. In fact, no pools in Palm Beach have screens.

Robert N. Wildrick

Resident

I love living in Palm Beach. It is my home and I miss it whenever I'm away.

Rush Limbaugh
Resident

The Kennedys were neighbors, and I was frequently invited to their home. One day my son and I had played doubles with John-John and a friend of his. Afterwards, John gave me a big hug and kiss before rushing off to catch his plane back to New York. My daughter Sasha, who was very young at the time, came running up to us with hands on her hips staring at John. He said, "You want a kiss, too"? She emphatically said "No!" I laughed all the way home and told her she'd just turned down the world's most eligible bachelor!

Dragana Connaughton

Resident

My favorite memory is of the visit in 1985 by the Prince and Princess of Wales for a benefit for United World Colleges. I was 17 years old. The day after the ball at The Breakers, the Shiny Sheet wrote that my friend Mary Frances Turner and I had run up and "attacked" Prince Charles. We found this hysterical and laughed at the images of us trying to get through his bodyguards. The truth was I had met the prince twice before, and he was very happy to graciously receive us both. Such a fabulous night!

Mara Goodman Davies

Resident

My favorite memory is the old pier at the foot of Worth Avenue, where we had so much down-to-earth fun fishing, surfing, eating breakfast and dancing.

My favorite thing to do here is surf with my dad and drive around admiring the greatest architecture in the world.

Edward Wright

The Trinity Collection

Beth Barber & friends

Palm Beach is one of the best and safest places in the world to live, work and play. We have enjoyed raising our children here. Palm Beach Day School provided them with an excellent education that helped them grow into thriving, successful adults. We love the lifestyle where we can laze by the pool, walk to the beach or to the bike path and enjoy the spectacular Florida weather. Palm Beach provides a variety of shopping and dining options to enjoy with the lifelong friends we've made here. After living in Palm Beach, we wouldn't live anywhere else!

Richard and Robin Bernstein

Resident

I love Palm Beach because it's the home of so many visionaries. Since 1921 when Palm Beach Day Academy was founded, leaders in the community have understood that our children are the future. I am blessed to head a school where a rare creative energy and commitment abound among members of our board of trustees, faculty, community at large, and parents.

Becky van der Bogert

Palm Beach Day Academy

July 4th 1976 was a momentous occasion on the island – our country's bicentennial. The morning was brutally hot and humid, with a few fluffy clouds. The ocean was like a turquoise lake. My wife, six months pregnant, and I stood under a shade tree in Bradley Park awaiting the unveiling of the new Gold Eagle statue at the north entrance to town. Ladies and gentlemen paraded around in period garb: men with skimmers and ladies with grandiose hats and parasols. Numerous antique autos from the 20s, 30s and 40s appeared, many driven by chauffeurs decked out in full uniforms.

Ralph Schenck

Newbridge Securities Corp.

Have you ever thought what it would be like to locate your business in Paradise? Then consider Palm Beach – we have it all. Weather, water, boats, architecture, education, high society, fashion, finance, bioscience, small government, golf, food and hospitality. And really nice people!! I have been blessed as President of the Palm Beach Business Group to cooperate with a number of town businesses for six years. I look forward to many more years in this very special community.

Tom Ross

Palm Beach Business Group, Inc.

Rhys Robinson, George Moss, Madeline Moss, Kit Spina,
Sydney Kosoy, Abby Moss, Marin Cvelbar

I feel blessed to live in Palm Beach, whether I'm lazing in my back yard, strolling on the sparkling walkway of wonderful Worth Avenue or walking the idyllic Lake Trail.

There's an indigenous peacefulness to the island's graceful palms, ficus and banyans; gentle lapping waves of shimmering Lake Worth, and in the springtime the fragrant scent of night-blooming jasmine caressing one's senses. Charming picturesque homes on coconut palm-lined streets and extraordinary cultural and architectural marvels abound along with wide boulevards with blossoming medians. This concoction of natural glories and human-made treasures renders Palm Beach the most beautiful town in the world.

Deborah C. Pollack
Resident

At midnight on New Year's Eve 2009, a neighbor's blind dog fell into the Intracoastal next to Ibis Isle where I live, and one of the neighbors risked his life to jump in and save it. I love that there are places here like Ibis, where people take care of each other (and their pets). Right now my husband, Paul Noble, is making chicken soup for a sick neighbor and I'm feeding another one's cat.

We "Ibisynnians" love our almost private park, and our pools, and individually all use the same word to describe this Palm Beach place: paradise.

Paulette Cooper Noble
Resident

I'm a native New Yorker who arrived in Palm Beach in the early 1960s. It was always a revelation to drive through town and be able to wave at friends on the streets.

After almost fifty years of paradise, I can't imagine living anywhere else. As a certified scuba diver with thousands of dives worldwide under my weight belt, our off-shore Gulf Stream diving is still to me the best in the world.

My dogs love the beach and share my love of the ocean. It would be difficult to improve on the perfection of the Palm Beach lifestyle.

Judy Schrafft
Resident

I just loved sail-fishing in Palm Beach on Sunday afternoons in the 1930s and 1940s. We caught and released hundreds... Wonderful, wonderful happy memories!

Kay Jordahn Rybovich
Resident

I've been fortunate enough to meet many presidents at the hotel. A few years ago President George H. W. Bush and his son Jeb arrived just as a crowd was leaving a Royal Room Cabaret performance. The crowd was elated, and one man called out, "I paid for a fabulous show with Lanie Kazan, and they threw in the President!" The Bushes were most gracious, shaking everyone's hands. It was a memorable moment that could only happen on our lovely island.

Ruth Young
The Colony

I came to Palm Beach in 2008 where I found a safe haven nestled between the Intracoastal Waterway and the ocean - friendly, happy people and lots of cats and dogs. This is a place where you can walk to the beach at midnight without fear - the way life should be. We have beautiful churches, a cobbler, bakeries, boutique hotels and a pharmacy with a lunch counter and the best shopping on Worth Avenue, South County Road and Royal Poinciana Way. This is a tight-knit community with open arms and soft hearts.

Denise B. Parisi

Denise B. Parisi, North of Worth

Sportscaster Curt Gowdy had a lot to do with moving my business from West Palm Beach to Palm Beach. We had become friends over the years and I'd go over to his house and smoke cigars and chat. He kept telling me that Palm Beach needed a high class vacuum shop. I already had a lot of customers from the island who arrived in Bentleys and Rolls Royces, so I decided to make the move. I'm really glad I took his advice. I've had a very warm welcome.

James W. Sim

All Brand Vacuums, Inc.

The thing I love about Palm Beach is that we're there for all the happy times! Music, good food, fine wine… It doesn't get any better than that!

Franny LaRue

Gourmet Galaxy

Terrence Smith on Lionheart

Ilove so much about the town – its amazing history, the inlet dock at sunset, the Worth Avenue renovation, even the newsprint used by the Shiny Sheet. I love the Old World feeling I get every time I walk into The Breakers, Mar-a-Lago and the Flagler Museum. The world's most interesting people often show up here. Most of all I love how this happens not by accident but because the people of the Town of Palm Beach have always acted to preserve that which we hold dear.

Michael Reiter
Resident

One day bestselling author Nelson DeMille called me saying he wanted me to give him a story about crime on the Island. What crime? In Palm Beach? Not much murder and mayhem here. Scott Fitzgerald, my hero, wrote a Palm Beach story called "The Offshore Pirate." Hmm. What about concocting a story about an "onshore pirate" where an Errol Flynn type arrives on his yacht every Season, steals from the rich, gives to...himself and call it..."The Pirate of Palm Beach!" Nelson loved it. First crime story inspired by...no crime!

Ted Bell

Resident

Growing up in Palm Beach was a fairy tale. We rode our bikes everywhere, including Anne's dock for a Coke from the machine. We'd walk from the inlet to the Worth Avenue pier on the beach, stopping at friends' houses for snacks. There was Perna's Ice Cream Shop, Hamburger Heaven for after school munchies and on Saturdays a movie at the Four Arts Theater just for kids. Later we enjoyed Christmas dances and the debutante ball where you danced all night with your father and favorite boyfriends.

Judy Testa

Testa's Palm Beach Restaurant

I remember when I lived in Palm Beach in the 50s and took my little boys to see the lighting of the Christmas tree which at that time was 5-6 feet tall. They were so excited!

Ann Tylander

Resident

I can still remember how cute Caroline and John John Kennedy were on Easter Sunday!

Mrs. Raymond J. Burke

Resident

When I was growing up I was told that in Palm Beach jeans were a no-no, and one should never chew gum. My Uncle Bob owned The Alibi and the Palm Beach Athletic Club and related great stories about people such as Rocky Marciano and Zsa Zsa Gabor. His advice to me: date someone on the other side of the bridge unless I wanted the whole town to know about it. And, of course, always live within walking distance of The Colony.

Judith LaFeir

Resident

The Michael Rose Orchestra had performed for years at Mar-a-Lago, so it was a thrill to be engaged on January 22, 2005 for "The Wedding of the Century" which inaugurated the new gilded Grand Ballroom built by Donald Trump for his bride Melania.

Our program consisted of specially written orchestrations representing the greatest love songs of the most important 20th century American composers, Gershwin, Porter, Kern, Rogers and Hammerstein, mixed with an assortment of classical pieces of Bach, Vivaldi and Mozart. The hall was filled with an overflow of notable invitees from every field of endeavor: entertainment, politics and sports.

Sandra and Michael Rose

Michael Rose Orchestra

From my experiences over the past thirty years, I have been increasingly impressed that people from all over the world attain a sense of place here in Palm Beach. Indeed, a great variety of personal expressions are all identified with this single, globally recognized location. And for us, it's been a great place to raise a family!

Bill Metzger

Resident

I love the ocean and palm trees on the Island - even after 35 years of working in Palm Beach.

Pam Henderson

The Rehabilitation Center for Children and Adults

We share an island graced by the legacy of inspired architects and amateur gardeners - a place where constantly surprising floral and bird life keep us tropical folk endlessly bewitched and amused.

Entertaining a blend of friends new and old, out of doors, rain or shine; small-town friendliness coupled with big town intellect in a picture-perfect setting - that's what has always made my family happy to call Palm Beach home.

Page Lee Hufty Bell

Resident

We just moved to Palm Beach last week. We are fixing up our new house. All the neighbors are so friendly. They say "stop over for a cup of vodka any time." We love it here in Palm Beach!!

Bruce Langmaid

Resident

I love the pride Palm Beach takes in its pets. We have a pet parade, fashion shows, and even a Pet Society book! My poodle Newman has many friends in town and is able to enjoy eating on the patio at many of our fine restaurants.

Randi Siegal

Rapunzel's Closet

I love the lack of pretension about Palm Beach, where pink and green are as chic as basic black, where knowing how to hold a conversation still matters, and surfing is something grown-ups do with as much passion as the kids! It is knowing that Lilly (Pulitzer) is just a few blocks away, gardening, reading, making people laugh, think, feel welcome. That is the essence of what makes this place so wonderful and special.

Cathy Orrico

C. Orrico

I've been in the banking business in Palm Beach since 1971, when the only banks in town were First National Bank of Palm Beach, Palm Beach National Bank & Trust and the Worth Avenue National Bank. You could walk down Worth Avenue and wave to Sara Frederick, Miss Martha, her daughter Lynn Manulis, Wally Findlay and Dr. Aldo Gucci as they strolled down the street.

Dr. Gucci was on the advisory board of my bank. He was funny, charming and wonderful. He seemed to always have a little "red sauce" on his tie.

Nancy Mizelle

Resident

Coming back from Duke to teach and coach some of the students who had been first graders when I graduated from the Palm Beach Day School was a great memory. Spending three years as an English teacher there while researching alumni and the history of the school, going back to 1921, and then founding the Alumni Association at the Day School, was a terrific experience. The Shiny Sheet records were where I found out the first schoolhouse for the Day School (formerly Palm Beach Private School), was actually down on Cocoanut Row between Royal Palm Way and Brazilian.

Scott Lewis

Scott Lewis' Gardening & Trimming

My favorite memories of Palm Beach are of the public tennis courts on Seaview Avenue, where I first played in the 1950s. In those days there were four green clay courts on the same site where there are now seven. For 40 years, until recently resurfaced, they were the best playing public courts anywhere.

James G. Pressly, Jr.
Resident

James G. Pressly, Jr.

I'm a car guy. I love car spotting in Palm Beach where one can see some of the most beautiful vehicles ever created. I love the Cavallino Classic event at The Breakers every January. I have entered my Ferraris in the event over the 18 years that I have been in Palm Beach. I love the bike trail, surfing with my son Jonathan at the flagpole beach and eating a hamburger with my wife, Aileen, at Cafe Boulud at the Brazilian Court Hotel.

Dr. Mitchell A. Josephs DDS

Palm Beach Dentist

D/E Brian LeBrun, Lt. Joe Sekula and F/F Caesar Mustelier
Palm Beach Fire Rescue

Officer Adam Zeller & Officer Michele D. Pagan

I moved to Palm Beach from Montreal in 1965 because one of my sons had Cystic Fibrosis. The theory was that salt air was beneficial for CF patients.

Soon I realized that philanthropy was a way of life here. With the help of the most generous, compassionate and loving people on the planet we founded the Palm Beach branch of the Cystic Fibrosis Foundation. Our signature event was the Sixty-Five Roses Ball, named when my young son, Richard, who heard me on the telephone a thousand times a day talking about cystic fibrosis, thought I was saying "Sixty-Five Roses".

Mary G. Weiss

Palm Beach Chapter, Cystic Fibrosis Foundation

Casa Apava

Residence of Mr. & Mrs. Dwight Schar

My wife, Louise, and I honeymooned here at the Whitehall Hotel in 1948. At that time I was earning $125 a week and spent just about all my savings on that honeymoon. If anyone had told me that one day we would be living here, I would have laughed it off as pure fantasy. Now we are here and actively engaged in this fabulous community. That is certainly a dream come true....only in America.

Michael Stein

Resident

I was inspired to start painting Palm Beach images when my late husband David Robinson Thompson and I rented a second floor apartment at 220 Australian Avenue. While interviewing him for a book I was writing, I looked beyond him and out the window to an inspiring and charming view of the tree-lined street and Brazilian Court Hotel. The way the foliage coalesced with the European architecture inspired artistic sensibilities and seemed to represent the essence of Palm Beach. I performed the painting, which became the first of over 350 images of the Island community where I own a gallery.

Sandra Thompson

Resident Artist

I have loved Palm Beach since I first visited it in the winter of 1958. I played golf at the Palm Beach Country Club and lunched at The Everglades Club. I found the town beautiful, its residents hospitable and the golf promising. I moved here permanently in the mid-1970s. Last week, my former wife Barbara and I lunched with all our children and grandchildren at Testa's. It felt the same as 1958. That's why I love it here.

Gerry Goldsmith

Resident

Sandra Thompson

One of my fondest memories of Palm Beach was attending live Broadway shows at the Royal Poinciana Theatre. I remember at age nine or ten my grandparents after the performance walking me across the street with my four sisters to Testa's for strawberry pie and crème de menthe parfaits. The actors and actresses from the show would autograph our playbooks then proceed to the bar for cocktails. I still have Van Johnson's signed Playbill in my library. It was an elegant, glamorous and gracious time.

Lawrence Moens
Resident

My favorite memory of Palm Beach is of the many evenings my husband Gene and I spent dining at Renato's. It felt like our own little corner of Tuscany, right in our backyard. I always ordered the filet of sole and Gene ordered pasta primavera; both were consistently superb. Luciano was our waiter, and he is still there bringing back memories of all the lovely times I spent with Gene. Whether we were enjoying a romantic dinner for two or a celebratory family dinner with the whole gang, Renato's was always the place to go.

Lois Pope

Resident

She's beautiful and lovely. Her body long and slim. With curves so inviting. Her outline always trim. Her favorite colors: blue and green. With sandy-coloured sash, but at the time of sunset, she wears an orange dress. Gardenias in her fair curls, Hibiscus at her foot, she stretches out a loving hand to everyone she'll meet. That's why I send this Valentine, for she's my happiness, but how to get these words to her, I don't have her address. By telling this to all of you, it will come within her reach, because-this Valentine, is for our sweet PALM BEACH.

Mary Hartree Ouwehand

Resident

I remember going with my mother Lillian Sheerr to what was then Charlie's Crab on Royal Poinciana Way, in the late 1940s or early 1950s. When we parked outside the restaurant we noticed we had a flat tire. A policeman came by and suggested we go and eat dinner and he'd have the tire fixed. When we finished dinner we found the car with a fixed tire and a nice note from the policeman.

I was so impressed with the small town atmosphere in Palm Beach that my husband and I moved here from New York 30 years later.

Muriel Kaplan
Resident

My favorite memory is spending time at The Breakers over the past 25 years. We loved letting our children throw pennies in the front fountain. All these years later our grandchildren are throwing pennies in the same fountain.

Sprinkles has been another focal point for our evening walks. A lot of blue Smurf ice cream consumed over the years! "Family" is the theme for us here. It began as our vacation spot, but now we consider it home.

Terri Schottenstein
Resident

Back in the late 1960s my dad Ed Foley was manager of The Breakers Beach and Golf Courses. Every morning we took our deposits to the bank, where they served orange juice and coffee in silver serving sets. I thought that was so elegant and classy and dreamed of the day I'd be involved in the business and cultural activities of the world's most famous island resort. Many balls at The Breakers and other social and political events later, I'm now living and working selling multi-million dollar real estate on the Island. Childhood dreams do come true.

Mark Foley

Former U.S. Congressman

Mark Foley and Michael Price

I remember my first Greater South County Road Association meeting that Jean Deyermond invited me to attend when I first met Jesse Newman and Mike Small. They were so kind to me the newcomer ... hard to believe that was about 18 years ago. What a great group of professionals working to improve South County Road businesses! It was about that time that the Foxtail Palms were being planted along South County Road with all kinds of festivities being planned. Now, so many years later I can't imagine the street without the palms. My thanks to the 1976 founders of Greater South County Road Association: Mike Small, Jesse Newman, Dede and Nigel Marix and Tom Keresey.

Patti Sans

President
Greater South County Road Association

In the 40s and 50s Palm Beach Day School, known as "Private," gave us two hours off for lunch to go to the Bath & Tennis Club or, in my case, to go home and practice piano. Most of us came on bicycles but others, such as the Vanderbilt girls, arrived in chauffeur-driven cars.

There was so much color in Palm Beach society back then that when a telegram arrived for Count von Ostheim without an address, the messenger boy was told to ask our father, Comte Henri de Marcellus, where he lived, as one count must know another.

Juliette de Marcellus

Resident

Cathy Orrico, Patti Sans, Amy Devore

When I was a little girl there were only two traffic lights in town, and they took them down in the summer because of hurricanes.

Helen Weigel

Patio and Bar Accessories

Palm Beach's history, stately elegance and endearing charm make it an exceptionally magical and extraordinary seaside gem. With its sensational glitz and glamour, it's the seasonal destination for the world's most elite, distinguished clientele as well as also being a very peaceful, serene and quiet town. The captivating mystique of Palm Beach provides a lovely setting to create long-lasting memories walking along the beach, shopping on Worth Avenue, meeting fascinating people and discovering new treasures all around the island.

Ellaina D. Tanos

Resident

Palm Beach has the most generous people in the world!

Dorothy A. Sullivan

Resident

The Lake Trail is a truly unique and wonderful feature of Palm Beach. The beautiful homes lining the path to the east and the downtown skyline to the west make this one of the most scenic places to walk, run and ride. It is both a place for exercise as well as greeting neighbors and visitors.

Kristy Pressly

Resident

The beauty of this island and its people resurrect memories of my Mediterranean roots. I am a big fan of Trevini Restaurant and Gianni and his staff, as they remind me of the warmth and passion of Italy and its charming cuisine. The allure and elegance that resides in every corner of this piece of "heaven on earth" is unparalleled. It is a joy to come to work every day with Palm Beach's breathtaking views and affable, savvy and distinctive residents.

Grace Halabi

BB&T

The Breakers Palm Beach

Founded in 1896 and listed on the National Register of Historic Places, The Breakers is an iconic oceanfront resort, renowned as one of the finest vacation destinations in North America. While respecting its rich heritage and tradition of unparalleled personalized service, The Breakers continuously invests in the ongoing revitalization and enhancement of its multi-faceted amenities to ensure guests every comfort and maintain the resort's appeal to future generations for years to come.

Guests of The Breakers enjoy the ultimate beachfront escape and the style and grace that only Palm Beach can provide. The Spa, acclaimed for its rejuvenating services, is just steps away from the soothing sounds of the Atlantic. The Mediterranean-style Beach Club and half-mile private beach are enhanced with lush landscaping, five sparkling pools, four whirlpool spas, and exclusive bungalows and cabanas. Guests can choose from 36 holes of championship golf, including The Breakers Rees Jones Course; 10 tennis courts; professional golf and tennis instruction; a variety of water sports; an interactive family entertainment center and kid's camp; nine distinctive restaurants ranging from casual to fine dining; 11 designer boutiques; and more.

For more information about The Breakers, visit thebreakers.com.
1-888-BREAKERS (273-2537)

A SALUTE TO PALM BEACH
WITH THANKS
FROM

THE FANJUL FAMILY

LAWRENCE A. MOENS ASSOCIATES, INC.

"SPECIALIZING IN PALM BEACHES FINEST RESIDENTIAL PROPERTIES"

Lawrence A. Moens Associates, Inc. is proud to be a Sponsor of the Palm Beach Centennial Book. Selling many of the important estates and fine properties on the Island for thirty-three years, our company has had the good fortune to flourish along with this very special community. We must be sure to preserve our town and our special quality of life as we enter the next one hundred years for our children and their children's children.

245 SUNRISE AVENUE, PALM BEACH, FLORIDA 33480
561.655.5510 / FAX 561.655.6744

THE HONORABLE LESLY S. SMITH

The William H. Pitt Foundation

The William H. Pitt Foundation was founded by William H. Pitt in 1986. Mr. Pitt was also the founder of William Pitt Real Estate in 1949, in Fairfield County Connecticut; a company which had a great impact on the development of Stamford, Connecticut and its surrounding communities. Mr. Pitt was a long-time member of the Palm Beach community where he made his home until his death in 2000. He was grateful for his great success in business and accordingly believed in giving back to the communities in which he lived and in developing future philanthropists. He said, "The best place to start building a strong community is with the young who need help". Today, The William H. Pitt Foundation Inc., carries on his legacy of giving. The Foundation's mission is to benefit or improve the lives, through education and other means, of deserving youth in Palm Beach County, Florida and Fairfield County, Connecticut. The Foundation has awarded scores of scholarship grants to young people and donated substantial endowments to area schools, hospitals and charitable organizations.

PALM BEACH DAILY NEWS

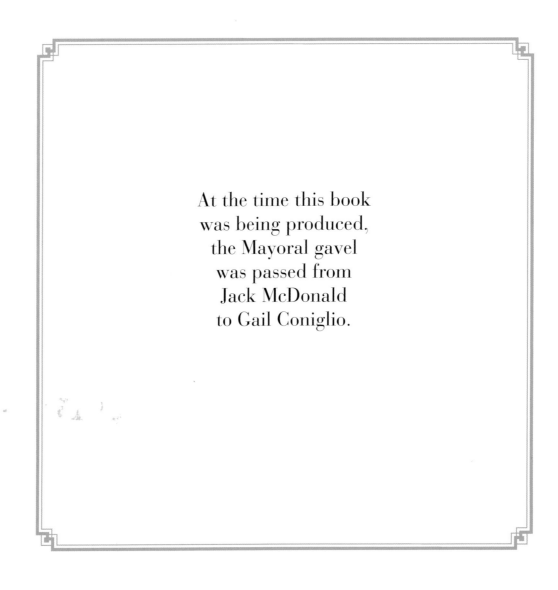

At the time this book
was being produced,
the Mayoral gavel
was passed from
Jack McDonald
to Gail Coniglio.